Hal Leonard Student Piano Library

Adult Piano Method

Popular Favorites
BOOK 1

Arranged by Fred Kern • Phillip Keveren • Mona Rejino

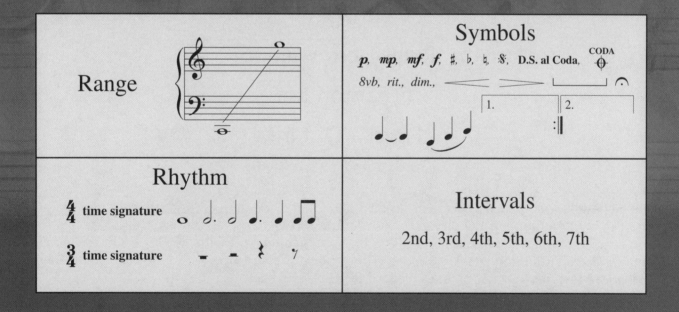

Range	Symbols
	p, *mp*, *mf*, *f*, ♯, ♭, ♮, 𝄋, D.S. al Coda, CODA
	8vb, *rit.*, *dim.*, 1. 2.

Rhythm	Intervals
4/4 time signature	2nd, 3rd, 4th, 5th, 6th, 7th
3/4 time signature	

ISBN 978-1-4234-9522-2

HAL•LEONARD®
CORPORATION
7777 W. BLUEMOUND RD. P.O. BOX 13819 MILWAUKEE, WI 53213

Visit Hal Leonard Online at
www.halleonard.com

Popular Favorites
BOOK 1

Suggested Order of Study:

The Nearness of You

Every Breath You Take

Don't Know Why

Help Me Make It Through the Night

Are You Lonesome Tonight?

I Hope You Dance

Bless the Broken Road

Imagine

Right Here Waiting

Lean on Me

From a Distance

 **TRACKS
1/2** The first track number is a practice tempo. The second track number is the performance tempo.

Contents

The Nearness of You

from the Paramount Picture ROMANCE IN THE DARK

Words by Ned Washington
Music by Hoagy Carmichael
Arranged by Mona Rejino

TRACKS
1/2

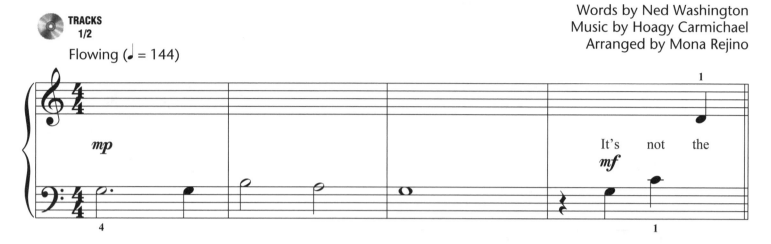

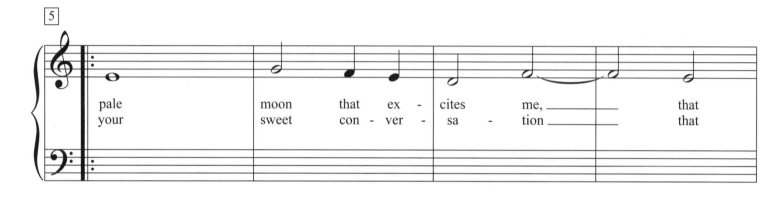

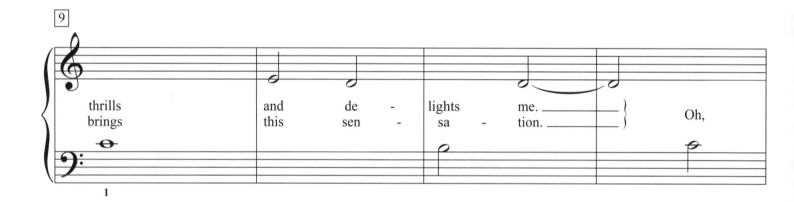

Accompaniment (Student plays one octave higher than written.)

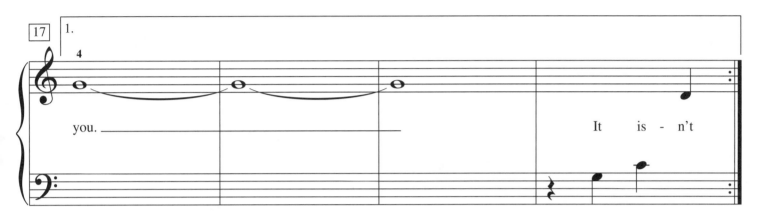

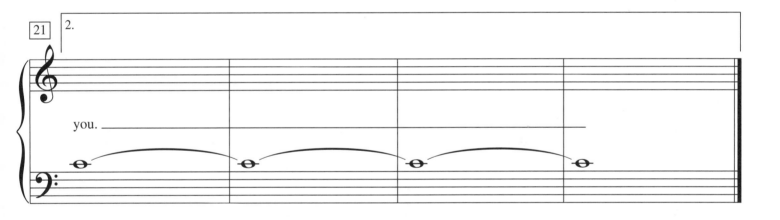

Every Breath You Take

Music and Lyrics by Sting
Arranged by Mona Rejino

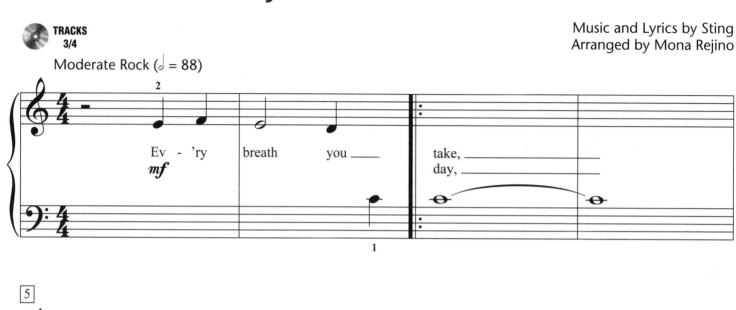

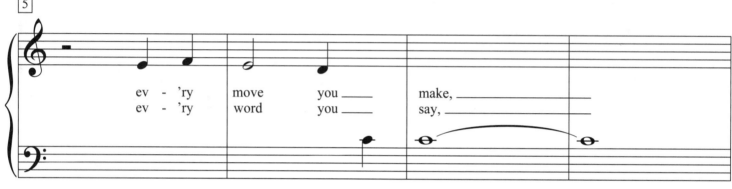

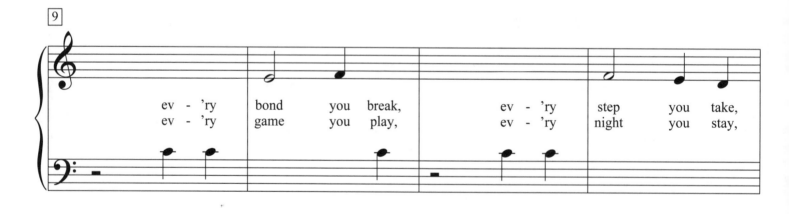

Accompaniment (Student plays one octave higher than written.)

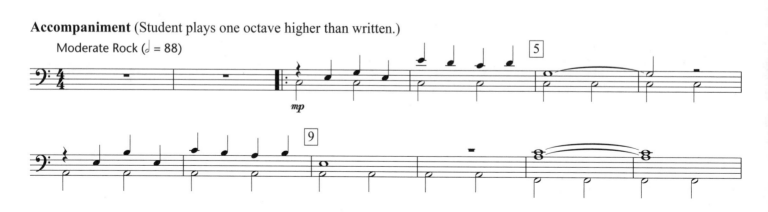

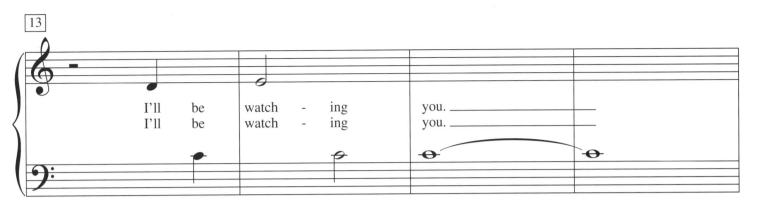

I'll be watch - ing you.
I'll be watch - ing you.

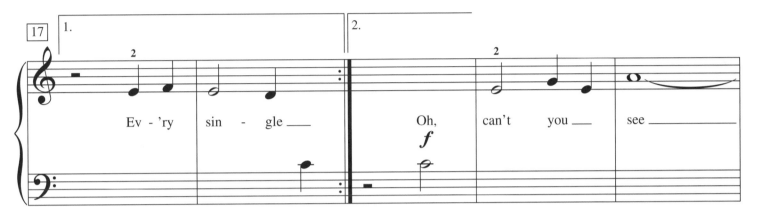

Ev - 'ry sin - gle

Oh, can't you see

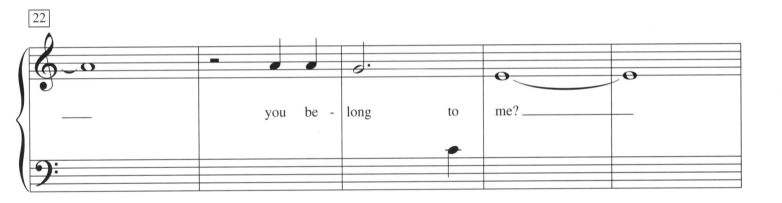

you be - long to me?

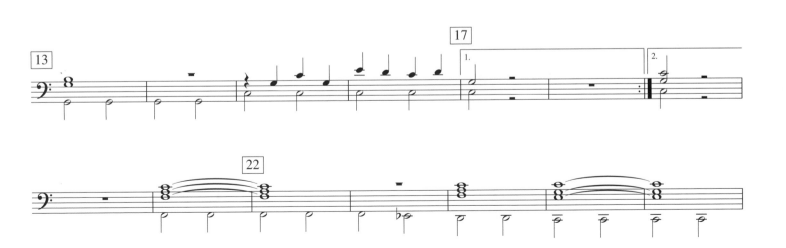

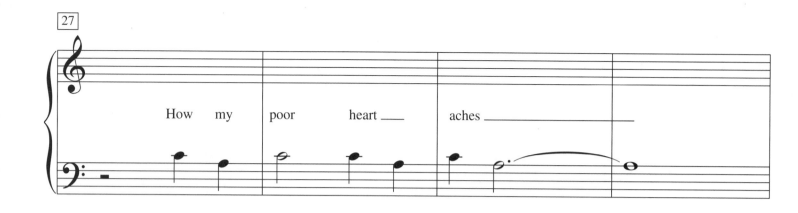

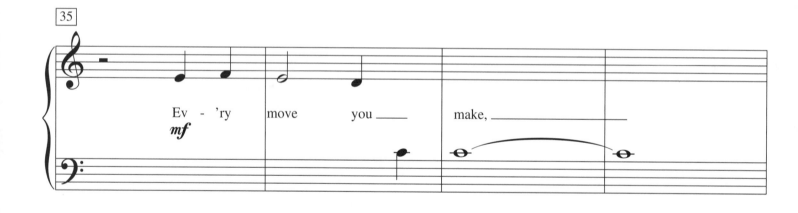

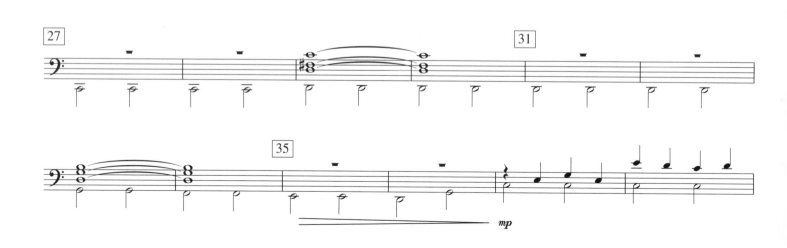

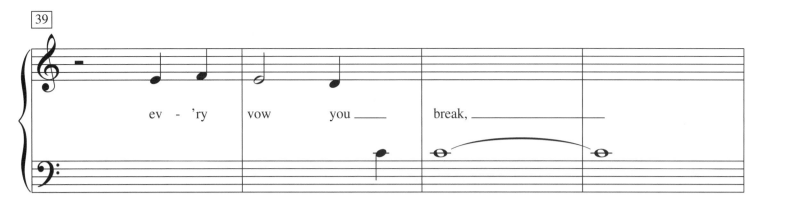

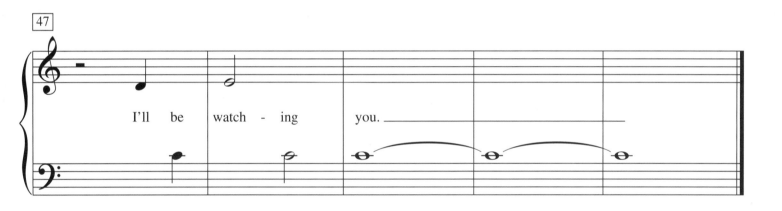

Don't Know Why

Words and Music by
Jesse Harris
Arranged by Phillip Keveren

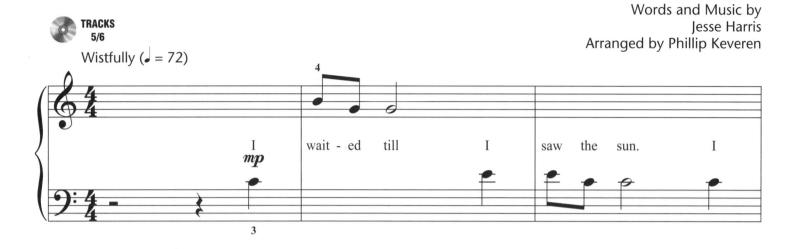

Accompaniment (Student plays one octave higher than written.)

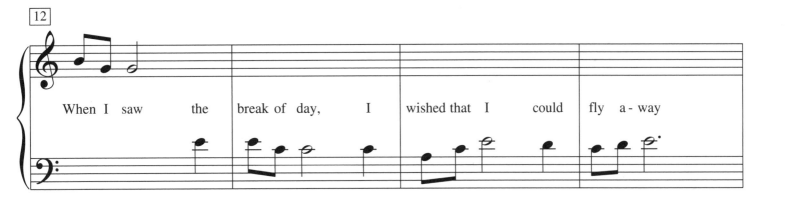

When I saw the break of day, I wished that I could fly a-way

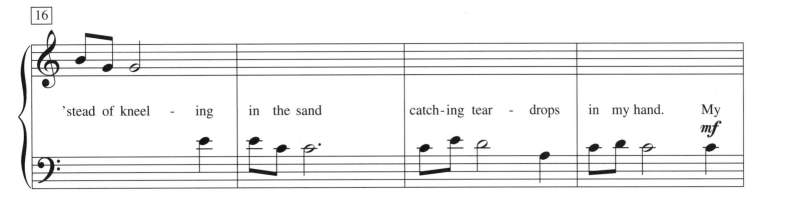

'stead of kneel - ing in the sand catch-ing tear - drops in my hand. My

mf

heart is drenched in wine, but you'll be

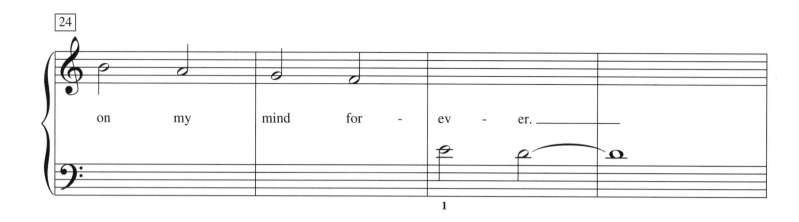

on my mind for - ev - er. _____

Out a-cross the end-less sea, I would die in ec - sta - sy.

mp

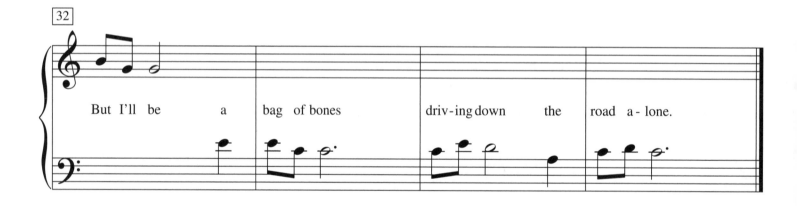

But I'll be a bag of bones driv-ing down the road a - lone.

Are You Lonesome Tonight?

Words and Music by Roy Turk
and Lou Handman

Accompaniment (Student plays one octave higher than written.)

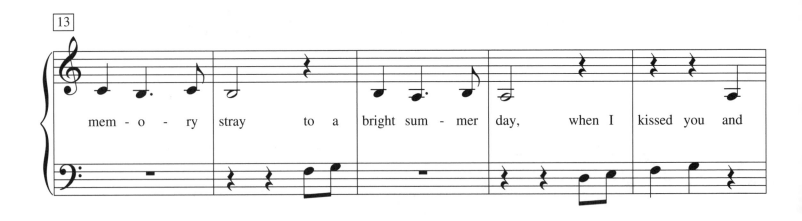

mem - o - ry stray to a bright sum - mer day, when I kissed you and

called you sweet - heart? _____ Do the chairs in your

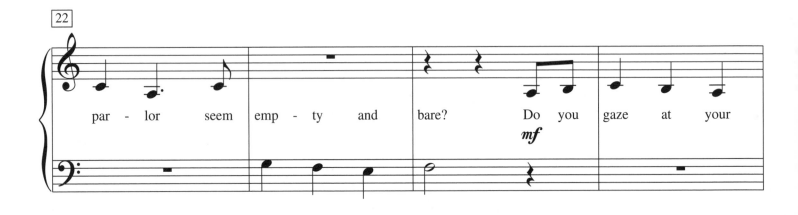

par - lor seem emp - ty and bare? Do you gaze at your

door - step and pic - ture me there? Is your heart filled with

pain, shall I come back a - gain? Tell me, dear, are you

f *mf*

1.

2.

lone - some to - night? Are you night?

mp

Help Me Make It Through the Night

Words and Music by
Kris Kristofferson
Arranged by Fred Kern

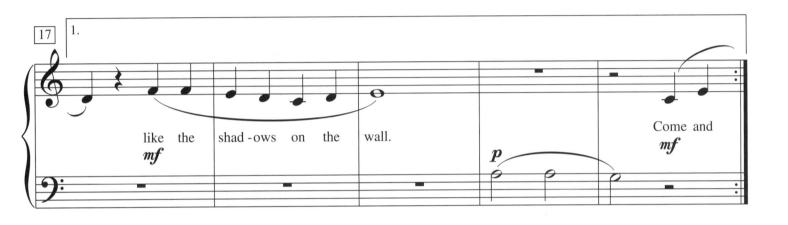

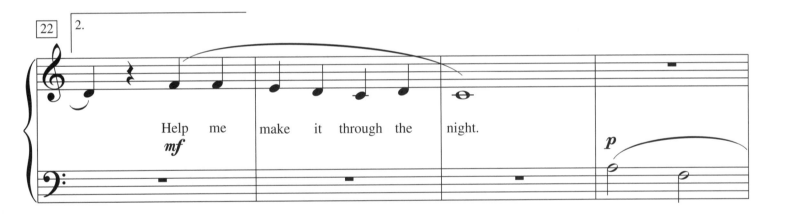

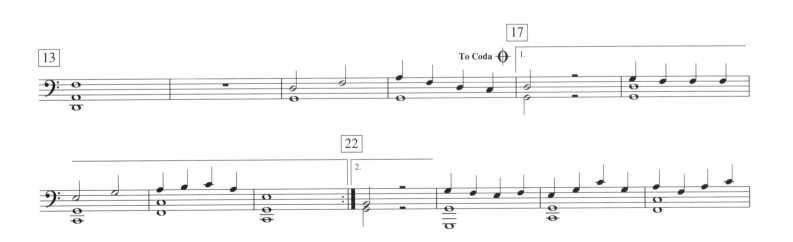

I don't care who's right or wrong,

I don't try to un - der - stand.

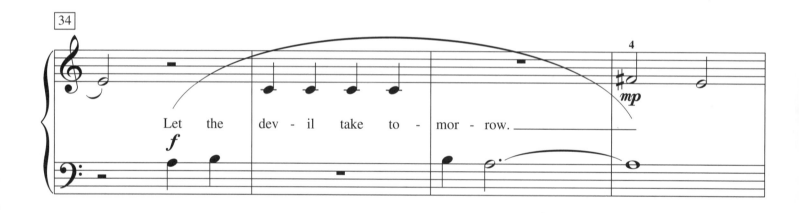

Let the dev - il take to - mor - row.

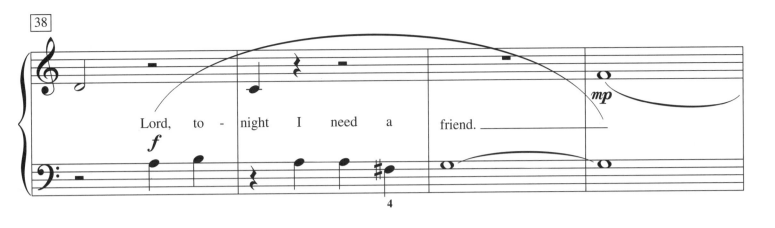

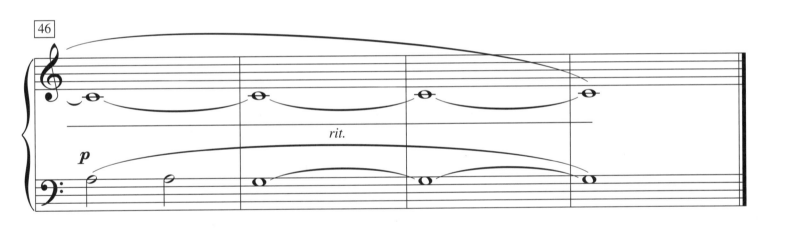

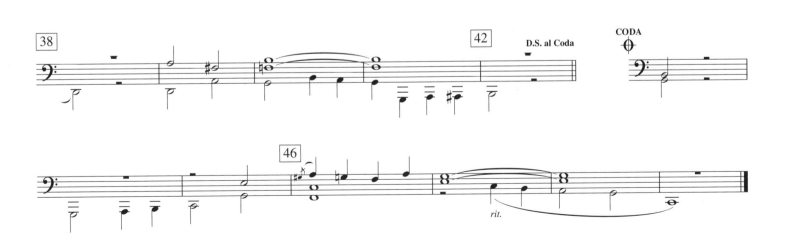

I Hope You Dance

Words and Music by Tia Sillers
and Mark D. Sanders
Arranged by Phillip Keveren

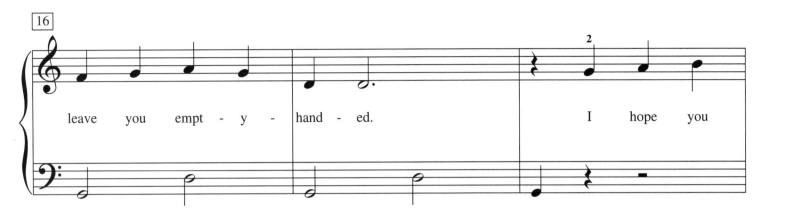

leave you empt - y - hand - ed. I hope you

still feel small when you stand be - side the o - cean.

When - ev - er one door clos - es, I hope one more o - pens.

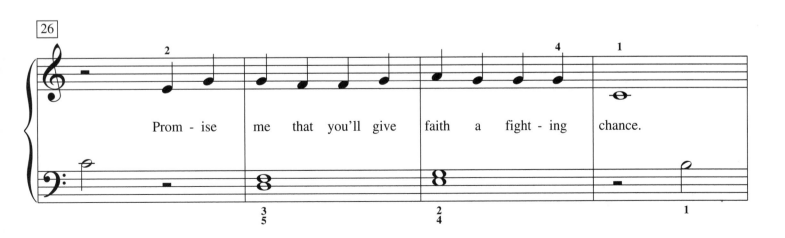

Prom - ise me that you'll give faith a fight - ing chance.

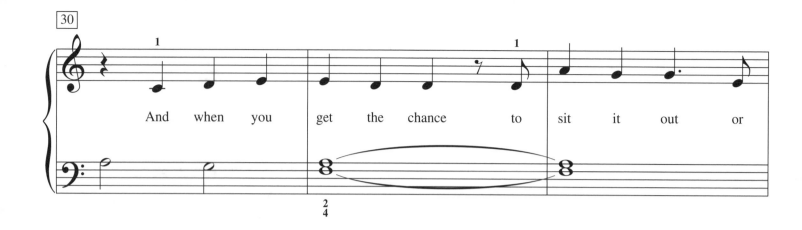

And when you get the chance to sit it out or

dance, I hope you dance.

I hope you dance.

I hope you dance.____

Bless the Broken Road

Words and Music by Marcus Hummon,
Bobby Boyd and Jeff Hanna
Arranged by Phillip Keveren

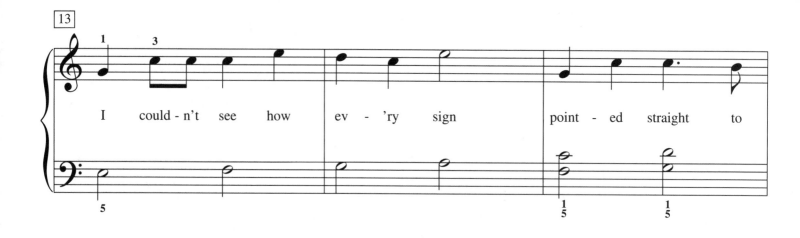

I could-n't see how ev-'ry sign pointed straight to

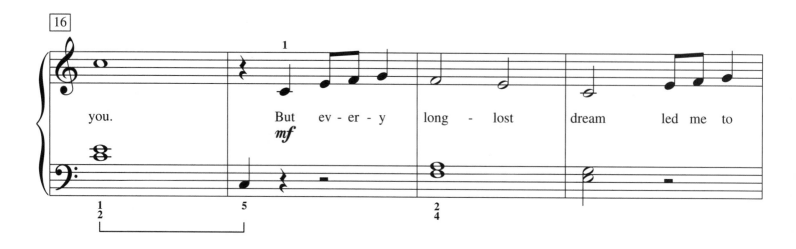

you. But ev-er-y long-lost dream led me to

where you are. Oth-ers who broke my

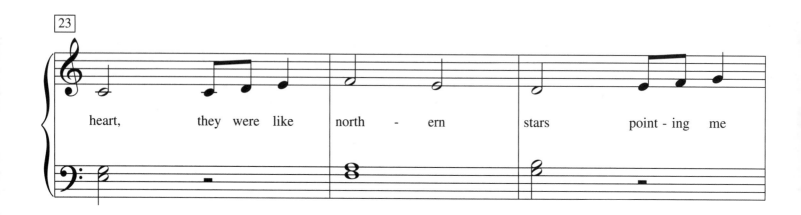

heart, they were like north-ern stars point-ing me

on my way in - to your lov - ing

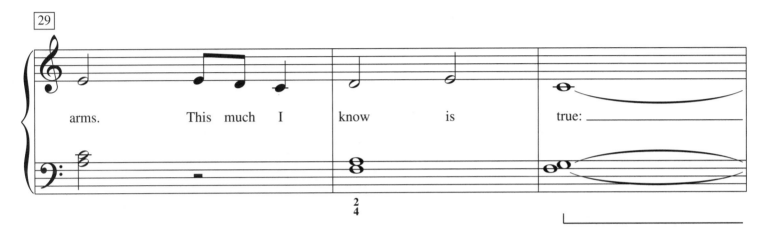

arms. This much I know is true:

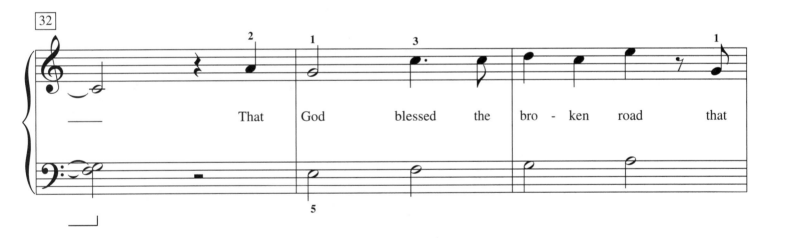

That God blessed the bro - ken road that

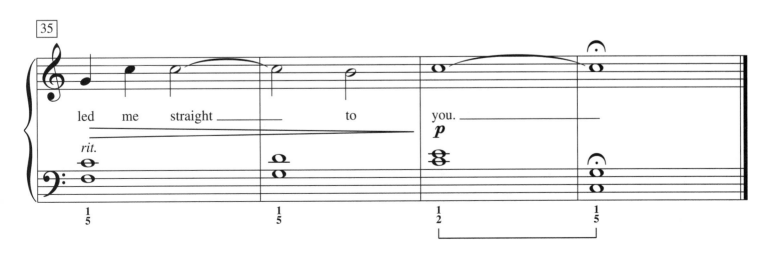

led me straight to you.

Imagine

Words and Music by
John Lennon
Arranged by Mona Rejino

I - mag - ine all the peo - ple _____ liv - ing for to - day. ___
I - mag - ine all the peo - ple _____ shar - ing all the world. _

_____ Ah. _____
_____ You, _____ you may say I'm a dream - er,

but I'm not the on - ly one. I hope some - day ___ you'll

join us ___ and the world ___ will live as one.

Right Here Waiting

Words and Music by
Richard Marx
Arranged by Mona Rejino

TRACKS 17/18

Moderately (♩ = 88)

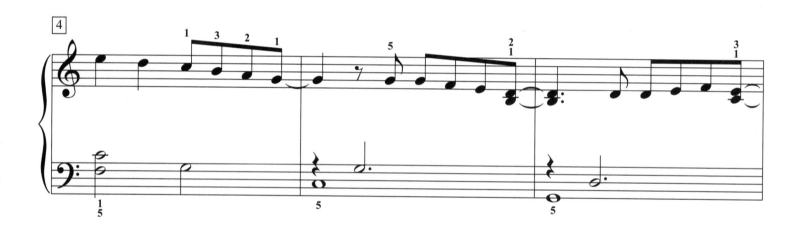

dim.

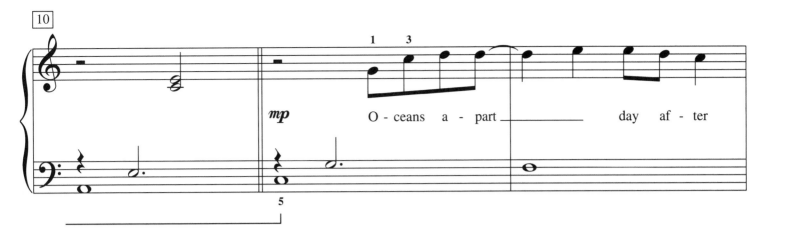

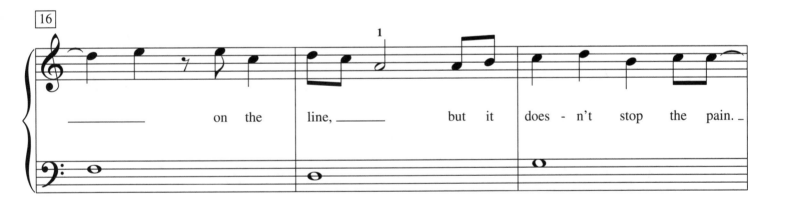

say for - ev - er? *mf* Wher - ev - er you go, —— what - ev - er you do, —

—— I will —— be right here wait - ing for you. What - ev - er it takes, —

—— or how my heart breaks, —— I will —— be right here wait - ing for you. —

dim. *rit.* *p*

30

Lean on Me

Words and Music by
Bill Withers
Arranged by Fred Kern

we know that there's al-ways to-mor - row. Lean on

me when you're not strong, I'll be your friend; I'll help you car-

- ry on, for it won't be long 'til I'm gon-na need

some-bod - y to lean on. Please swal-low your pride

if I have things ___ you need to bor - row, ___

for no one can fill ___ those of your needs ___ that you won't let ___

show. ___ You just call on me, broth- er, when you need a hand. ___ We all

need some-bod - y to lean ___ on. ___ I just might have a prob-lem that

you'll un-der-stand. _ We all need some-bod-y to lean _____ on. _ Lean on

me when you're not strong, _ I'll be your friend; _ I'll help you car-

-ry on, _____ for it won't be long _ 'til I'm gon-na need _

___ some-bod-y to lean _ on. _ You just _ on. _

From a Distance

Words and Music by
Julie Gold
Arranged by Fred Kern

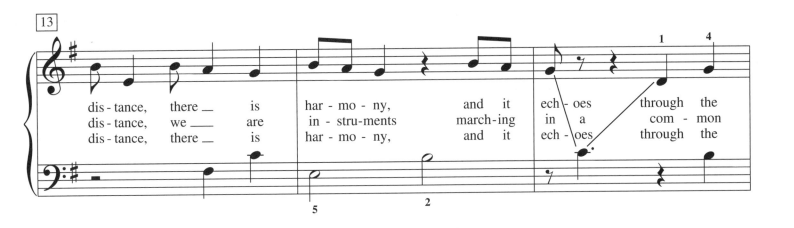

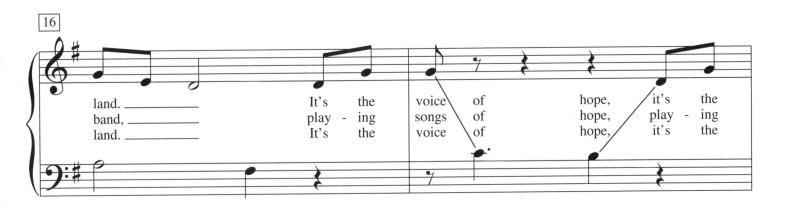

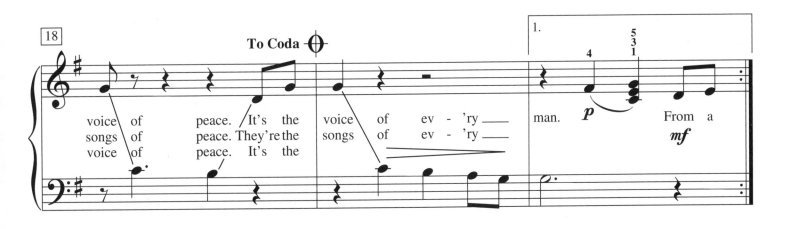

watch-ing us from a dis-tance. God is watch-ing us. God is

D.S. al Coda

watch-ing us. God is watch-ing us from a dis - tance. _____ From a

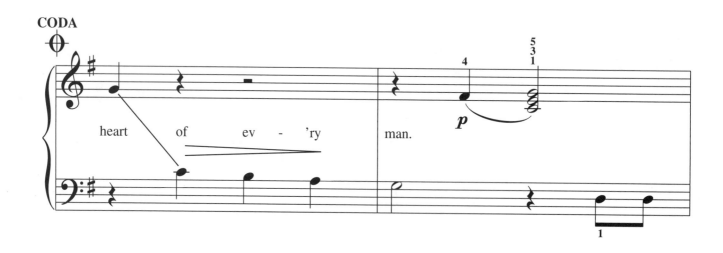

CODA

heart of ev - 'ry man.

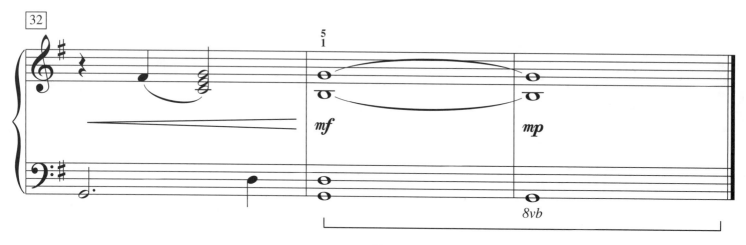

8vb

Hal Leonard Student Piano Library

Adult Piano Method

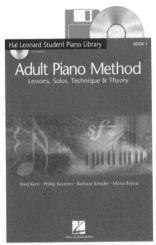

Adult Piano Method

Adults want to play rewarding music and enjoy their piano study. They deserve a method that lives up to those expectations. The new *Hal Leonard Student Piano Library Adult Piano Method* does just that and more.

Method Book 1
00296441 Book/CD $16.99
00296442 Book/GM Disk $16.95

Method Book 2
00296480 Book/CD $16.99
00296481 Book/GM Disk $16.95

Popular Hits Book 1

Our hit-packed supplementary songbook includes these titles: American Pie • Circle of Life • Fun, Fun, Fun • Let It Be Me • Murder, She Wrote • The Music of the Night • My Heart Will Go On • Sing • Strangers in the Night • Vincent (Starry Starry Night) • Y.M.C.A. • The Way You Look Tonight.

00296541 Book/CD $12.99
00296542 Book/GM Disk $12.95

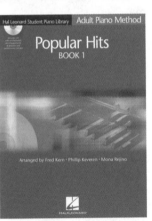

Popular Hits Book 2

12 hits: I Will Remember You • I Wish You Love • I Write the Songs • In the Mood • Moon River • Oh, Pretty Woman • The Phantom of the Opera • Stand by Me • Tears in Heaven • Unchained Melody • What a Wonderful World • When I'm Sixty-Four.

00296652 Book/CD $12.99
00296653 Book/GM Disk $12.95

Christmas Favorites Book 1

12 favorites: Away in a Manger • Deck the Hall • God Rest Ye Merry, Gentlemen • I Saw Three Ships • Jingle Bells • Joy to the World • O Come, O Come, Emmanuel • O Little Town of Bethleham • Silent Night • Ukrainian Bell Carol • We Wish You a Merry Christmas • What Child Is This?

00296544 Book/CD Pack...$12.95
00296547 Book/GM Disk $12.95

Christmas Favorites Book 2

12 more holiday classics: Angels We Have Heard on High • Bring a Torch, Jeannette Isabella • Dance of the Sugar Plum Fairy • Ding Dong! Merrily on High! • The First Noel • Go, Tell It on the Mountain • Hark! The Herald Angels Sing • The Holly and the Ivy • O Christmas Tree • O Holy Night • Still, Still, Still • We Three Kings of Orient Are.

00296668 Book/CD Pack...$12.99
00296669 Book/GM Disk $12.95

Traditional Hymns, Book 1

16 sacred favorites: All Glory, Laud and Honor • Come, Thou Almighty King • For the Beauty of the Earth • Holy, Holy, Holy! • It Is Well with My Soul • Joyful, Joyful, We Adore Thee • A Mighty Fortress Is Our God • What a Friend We Have in Jesus • and more.

00296782 Book/CD Pack...$12.99

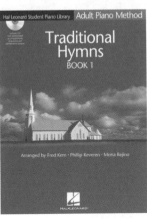

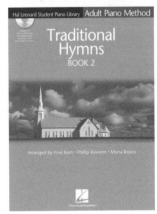

Traditional Hymns Book 2

15 more traditional hymns: All Things Bright and Beautiful • Ezekiel Saw the Wheel • God of Grace and God of Glory • God Will Take Care of You • In the Garden • Lord, I Want to Be a Christian • Stand Up, Stand Up for Jesus • Swing Low, Sweet Chariot • This Is My Father's World • and more.

00296783 Book/CD Pack...$12.99

Prices, contents and availability subject to change without notice.

FOR MORE INFORMATION, SEE YOUR LOCAL MUSIC DEALER,
OR WRITE TO:

HAL•LEONARD® CORPORATION
7777 W. BLUEMOUND RD. P.O. BOX 13819 MILWAUKEE, WI 53213

www.halleonard.com

POPULAR SONGS
HAL LEONARD STUDENT PIANO LIBRARY

The **Hal Leonard Student Piano Library** has great songs, and you will find all your favorites here: Disney classics, Broadway and movie favorites, and today's top hits. These graded collections are skillfully and imaginatively arranged for students and pianists at every level, from elementary solos with teacher accompaniments to sophisticated piano solos for the advancing pianist.

  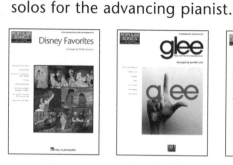    

The Beatles
arr. Eugénie Rocherolle

Intermediate piano solos. Songs: *Can't Buy Me Love • Get Back • Here Comes the Sun • Martha My Dear • Michelle • Ob-La-Di, Ob-La-Da • Revolution • Yesterday.*
00296649 Correlates with HLSPL Level 5.........$10.99

Broadway Hits
arr. Carol Klose

Early-Intermediate/Intermediate piano solos. Songs: *Beauty and the Beast • Circle of Life • Do-Re-Mi • It's a Grand Night for Singing • The Music of the Night • Tomorrow • Where Is Love? • You'll Never Walk Alone.*
00296650 Correlates with HLSPL Levels 4/5 .....$6.95

Chart Hits
arr. Mona Rejino

8 pop favorites carefully arranged at an intermediate level. Songs: *Bad Day • Boston • Everything • February Song • Home • How to Save a Life • Put Your Records On • What Hurts the Most.*
00296710 Correlates with HLSPL Level 5......... $7.99

Christmas Cheer
arr. Phillip Keveren

Early Intermediate level. For 1 Piano/4 Hands. Songs: *Caroling, Caroling • The Christmas Song • It Must Have Been the Mistletoe • It's Beginning to Look like Christmas • Rudolph the Red-Nosed Reindeer • You're All I Want for Christmas.*
00296616 Correlates with HLSPL Level 4...........$6.95

Christmas Time Is Here
arr. Eugénie Rocherolle

Intermediate level. For 1 piano/4 hands. Songs: *Christmas Time Is Here • Feliz Navidad • Here Comes Santa Claus (Right Down Santa Claus Lane) • I'll Be Home for Christmas • Little Saint Nick • White Christmas.*
00296614 Correlates with HLSPL Level 5...........$7.99

Classic Joplin Rags
arr. Fred Kern

Intermediate/Late Intermediate. Six quintessential Joplin rags arranged by Fred Kern: *Bethena (Concert Waltz) • The Entertainer • Maple Leaf Rag • Pineapple Rag • Pleasant Moments (Ragtime Waltz) • Swipesy (Cake Walk).*
00296743 Correlates with HLSPL Level 5......... $6.95

Contemporary Movie Hits
arr. by Carol Klose, Jennifer Linn and Wendy Stevens

Six blockbuster movie favorites arranged for intermediate-level piano solo: *Bella's Lullaby • Breaking Free • Dawn • Georgiana • He's a Pirate • That's How You Know.*
00296780 Correlates with HLSPL Level 5.......... $8.99

Current Hits
arr. Mona Rejino

Seven of today's hottest hits by artists such as Coldplay, Daughtry and Leona Lewis arranged as intermediate solos. Includes: *Apologize • Bleeding Love • Bubbly • Love Song • No One • Viva La Vida • What About Now.*
00296768 Correlates with HLSPL Level 5.......... $8.99

Disney Favorites
arr. Phillip Keveren

Late-Elementary/Early-Intermediate piano solos. Songs: *Beauty and the Beast • Circle of Life • A Dream Is a Wish Your Heart Makes • I'm Late; Little April Shower • A Whole New World (Aladdin's Theme) • You Can Fly! • You'll Be in My Heart.*
00296647 Correlates with HLSPL Levels 3/4 .....$9.99

Getting to Know You –
Rodgers & Hammerstein Favorites

Illustrated music book. Elementary/Late Elementary piano solos with teacher accompaniments. Songs: *Bali H'ai • Dites-Moi (Tell Me Why) • The Farmer and the Cowman • Getting to Know You • Happy Talk • I Whistle a Happy Tune • I'm Gonna Wash That Man Right Outa My Hair • If I Loved You • Oh, What a Beautiful Mornin' • Oklahoma • Shall We Dance? • Some Enchanted Evening • The Surrey with the Fringe on Top.*
00296613 Correlates with HLSPL Level 3 ....$12.95

Glee
arr. Jennifer Linn

Jennifer Linn provides intermediate-level solo arrangments of seven favorites from *Glee*: *Don't Stop Believin' • Endless Love • Imagine • Jump • Lean on Me • Proud Mary • True Colors.*
00296834 Correlates with HLSPL Level 5 ....$10.99

Elton John
arr. Carol Klose

8 classic Elton John songs arranged as intermediate solos: *Can You Feel the Love Tonight • Candle in the Wind • Crocodile Rock • Goodbye Yellow Brick Road • Sorry Seems to Be the Hardest Word • Tiny Dancer • Written in the Stars • Your Song.*
00296721 Correlates with HLSPL Level 5 ....$7.95

Joplin Ragtime Duets
arr. Fred Kern

Features full-sounding, intermediate-level arrangements for one piano, four hands of: *Heliotrope Bouquet • Magnetic March • Peacherine Rag • The Ragtime Dance.*
00296771 Correlates with HLSPL Level 5 .... $7.99

Jerome Kern Classics
arr. Eugénie Rocherolle

Intermediate level. Students young and old will relish these sensitive stylings of enduring classics: *All the Things You Are • Bill • Can't Help Lovin' Dat Man • I've Told Ev'ry Little Star • The Last Time I Saw Paris • Make Believe • Ol' Man River • Smoke Gets in Your Eyes • The Way You Look Tonight • Who?*
00296577 Correlates with HLSPL Level 5 .... $12.99

Melody Times Two
Classic Counter-Melodies for
Two Pianos, Four Hands
arr. Eugénie Rocherolle

This collection of classic counter-melody songs features four elegant and thoroughly entertaining arrangements for two pianos, four hands. Includes a definition and history of counter-melodies throughout musical periods; song histories; and composer biographies. The folio includes two complete scores for performance. Intermediate Level 4 Duos: *Baby, It's Cold Outside • Play a Simple Melody • Sam's Song • (I Wonder Why?) You're Just in Love.*
00296360 Intermediate Duets $12.95

Movie Favorites
arr. Fred Kern

Early-Intermediate/Intermediate piano solos. Songs: *Forrest Gump (Feather Theme) • Hakuna Matata • My Favorite Things • My Heart Will Go On • The Phantom of the Opera • Puttin' On the Ritz • Stand by Me.*
00296648 Correlates with HLSPL Levels 4/5 .....$6.99

Sing to the King
arr. Phillip Keveren

These expressive arrangements of popular contemporary Christian hits will inspire and delight intermediate-level pianists. Songs include: *By Our Love • Everlasting God • In Christ Alone • Revelation Song • Sing to the King • Your Name • and more.*
00296808 Correlates with HLSPL Level 5 .... $8.99

Sounds of Christmas (Volume 3)
arr. Rosemary Barrett Byers

Late Elementary/Early Intermediate level. For 1 piano/4 hands. Songs: *Blue Christmas • Christmas Is A-Comin' (May God Bless You) • I Saw Mommy Kissing Santa Claus • Merry Christmas, Darling • Shake Me I Rattle (Squeeze Me I Cry) • Silver Bells.*
00296615 Correlates with HLSPL Levels 3/4 .....$7.99

Today's Hits
arr. Mona Rejino

Intermediate-level piano solos. Songs: *Bless the Broken Road • Breakaway • Don't Know Why • Drops of Jupiter (Tell Me) • Home • Listen to Your Heart • She Will Be Loved • A Thousand Miles.*
00296646 Correlates with HLSPL Level 5...........$7.99

You Raise Me Up
arr. Deborah Brady

Contemporary Christian favorites. Elementary-level arrangements. Optional teacher accompaniments add harmonic richness. Songs: *All I Need • Forever • Open the Eyes of My Heart, Lord • We Bow Down • You Are So Good to Me • You Raise Me Up.*
00296576 Correlates with HLSPL Levels 2/3 .....$7.95

FOR MORE INFORMATION, SEE YOUR LOCAL MUSIC DEALER, OR WRITE TO:

HAL•LEONARD®
CORPORATION
7777 W. BLUEMOUND RD. P.O. BOX 13819 MILWAUKEE, WI 53213

Prices, contents and availability subject to change without notice. Prices may vary outside the U.S.

Disney characters and artwork © Disney Enterprises, Inc.

Visit our web site at **www.halleonard.com/hlspl.jsp** for all the newest titles in this series and other books in the Hal Leonard Student Piano Library.